30 DAILY DEVOTIONS

WHAT'S IN YOUR LOCKER?

Cover photo: Kerri Herner
Art direction and design: Rule29
Editor: Dale Reeves
Project Editor: Lindsay Black

Library of Congress Cataloging-in-Publication Data:

Kast, Michael, 1966-
    What's in your locker? : 30 daily devotions / Michael Kast.-- 2nd ed.
        p. cm.
    "Empowered Youth Products."
        Includes bibliographical references and index.
    ISBN 0-7847-1774-5 (pbk.)
1. High school students--Prayer-books and devotions--English. 2. Christian teenagers--Prayer-books and devotions--English. 3. Devotional calendars. I. Title.

BV4850.K375 2005
242'.63--dc22

2005007261

12   11   10   09   08   07   06   05   7   6   5   4   3   2   1

ISBN 0-7847-1774-5

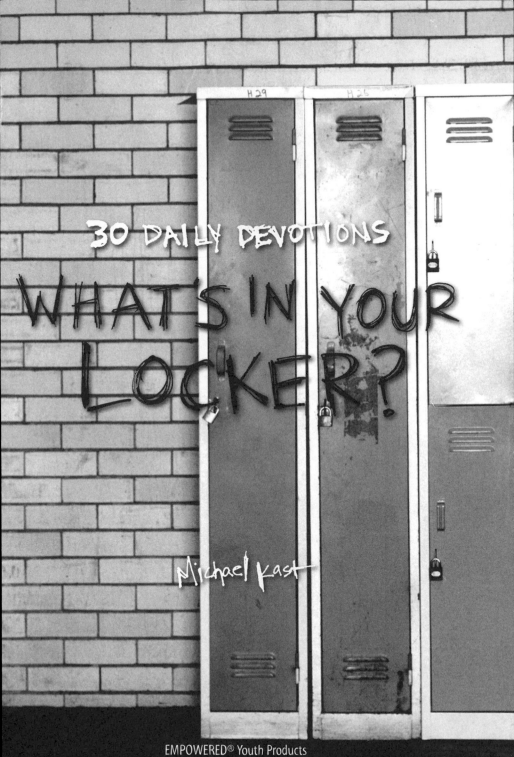

30 DAILY DEVOTIONS

WHAT'S IN YOUR LOCKER?

Michael Kast

EMPOWERED® Youth Products
Standard Publishing | Cincinnati, Ohio

DEDICATION

This book is dedicated to my lifelong sweetheart, my best friend, my wife and the mother of our children, Jill Kast. Thanks for helping me keep my locker in order.

CONTENTS

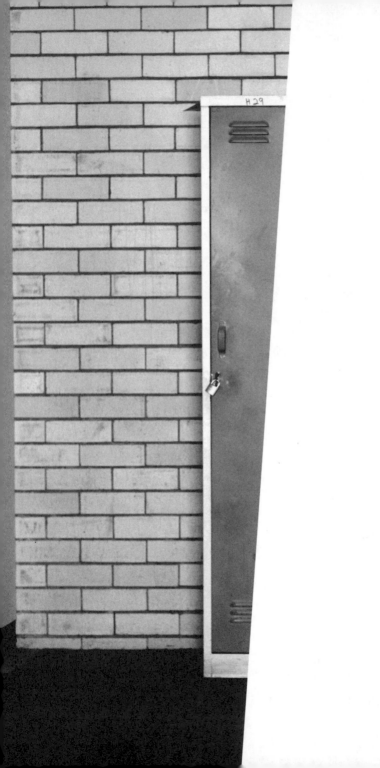

INTRODUCTION

Your school locker is much more than just a place to store your books and coat. It's one of the few places in the world that you can call your own—for a semester anyway. You are free to keep it as clean or messy as you please, as long as it doesn't pose a health hazard. You can decorate it to fit your personality. You can add shelves, mirrors and stickers—just about anything you want.

In fact, over the course of the year, your locker will take on your personality. If you are particular, you'll keep it clean. If you don't really care, it'll be a mess. You can advertise your favorite sports team, radio station, top 40 band and current boyfriend or girlfriend.

Your locker says a lot about who you are. It speaks about your priorities, likes, dislikes, interests and sometimes your beliefs.

The goal of this book is to be a daily devotional guide for you. Each day you'll read a short devotion that will take a look at different items found in lockers. Things like a mirror, pictures, a jacket, gym clothes, CDs, notes from a friend and money. Each of these items says something about you.

HOW TO USE THIS BOOK

This book is not designed to be read in one sitting. In fact, it is intended for you to read one chapter a day and be able to think about just one aspect of your life each day for thirty days.

Getting started

Just by having this book, you have taken a huge step. Whether you bought it on your own, or it was given to you as a gift, you are on the edge of a great adventure with God. Don't put it off any longer—dive right in.

Pick a time

View this time as an appointment with God. If you forget, you are breaking your promise to God that you'd meet with him. Don't forget—he's always there for you and will never break his appointment with you.

Pick a place

Think about a place where you can spend ten to fifteen uninterrupted minutes concentrating on your relationship with God. Maybe that's in your room, or maybe it's at the breakfast table. Wherever it is, claim it as your special place where you will come to meet God each day.

Get ready

As you go through this book, you will need a Bible and something to write with. Before you start, spend some time asking God to help you keep your appointment. Ask him to make this time valuable for you so that you can walk away each day with one area to think about throughout the day.

Each day

You will need to set aside about ten to fifteen minutes for each day. Each devotion includes a journaling space for your thoughts. HITTING THE BOOK will help you answer the question, "What does God have to say to me today?" LESSONS LEARNED will help you respond to the question, "What does he want me to learn today?" TODAY'S ASSIGNMENT will help you deal with the question, "What does he want me to do today?" TALKING TO GOD allows you to write out your prayer thoughts for the day.

I want to encourage you to be open and honest with yourself and God as you work your way through this book. No one will see this but you, unless you choose to show it to someone. The next time you open your locker and see everything that's in there, don't just think about getting to your next class. Be reminded that your locker is full of lessons from God to help get you through the day.

DAY 1 | BOOKS
Know God's commands

The reason that lockers were first installed in schools was to provide a place for students to keep their books while they were away from school or in class. Even though lockers are filled with other things, storing schoolbooks is still the main reason students have lockers today.

There is something special about schoolbooks. Left behind by students who have used them in years past, they all have a history. Students have written their names on the front page, and they may have highlighted important items when studying for a test. When you hold that book in your hands, you hold a little bit of history.

Your schoolbooks contain the information that you are going to cover in the upcoming semester. That information is presented to increase your knowledge. This newfound knowledge will help you as you go through life. Having knowledge is important, but having the right knowledge is of paramount importance.

I know a guy named Dan who decided—for no apparent reason—that he was not going to use any of his books all semester. He took great pride in stacking them in the bottom of his locker, and he bragged about never taking them to class or home to study. At first he didn't have much trouble. If he needed to read something for a test, he'd just borrow someone else's book and read it. If he needed to do math homework, he'd copy the problems down and do the work at home.

But as the semester rolled on, it got harder and harder for Dan to make it through without his books. His friends got tired of loaning him their books just so he could reach his ludicrous goal.

It wasn't long before his grades began to drop and his teachers heard about his plan. Soon the teachers began making him bring his books to class.

It's pretty obvious that this guy was a little odd. Dan made life tough on himself and his friends. He also missed out on some of the helpful information his schoolbooks contained.

HITTING THE BOOK

Having the right knowledge is important in almost every situation, and God wants to give it to us. In Psalm 119:66 King David says, "Teach me knowledge and good judgment, for I believe in your commands." In Proverbs 8:10 Solomon writes, "Choose my instruction instead of silver, knowledge rather than choice gold." What do these verses say to you?

LESSONS LEARNED

What do you think God is trying to tell you from his Word today?
Which of God's guidelines do you have a hard time following?

_____

_____

_____

_____

_____

_____

_____

_____

_____

_____

TODAY'S ASSIGNMENT

How can you act on this life lesson today? What can you do to get
more knowledge?

_____

_____

_____

_____

_____

_____

_____

_____

TALKING TO GOD

Take a few minutes to ask God to help you carry this lesson with you throughout the day. What do you need to say to him today?

_____

_____

_____

_____

_____

_____

_____

_____

_____

_____

OTHER THOUGHTS

_____

_____

_____

_____

_____

_____

_____

_____

_____

DAY 2 | MIRROR
God looks at your heart

After all the hassles that you go through in the morning—getting out of bed, getting ready for school and actually getting to school—it's amazing that you make it to school on time. That's why one of the greatest features of every locker is that it has a door—the perfect spot to hang a mirror. Locker mirrors have been known to save students from huge embarrassment on more than one occasion.

You may be among the many who stumble out of bed and get ready fairly quickly. Your senses aren't entirely focused, and when you rush out of the house in the morning, it's easy to miss something—a button on your shirt, a little dried toothpaste on your lip, a new zit or bed-head hair. Thankfully, when you get to school, you can check yourself in a locker mirror and catch any major mistakes before everyone sees them and has a laugh at your expense.

It's important to try to look presentable, but sometimes we are way too concerned with our appearances. I went to school with a guy named Matt who used to spend twenty minutes combing his hair after gym class. He'd comb and comb and comb to get it just right. He'd use his brush, blow dryer and tons of hair spray. When he was satisfied, he'd head toward the door, but just before he left the locker room, he'd put on his baseball cap. All of us in the locker room would shake our heads in disbelief because he'd just spent so much time being concerned with his hair, and within minutes he'd have hat-head.

The way we look is very important to us. We spend time each day making sure that we look our best. The way people look can say a lot about who they are and how they feel about themselves—but appearances can be misleading. Sometimes we jump to conclusions about other people based on the clothes they wear, the style of their hair, the shape of their bodies—and that's just the beginning of a potentially infinite list. Occasionally those snap judgments are dead-on, but more often than not, they're off base and potentially hurtful. Fortunately for us, God doesn't judge us based on how we look or how many school activities we're involved in—he's concerned with what's in our hearts.

HITTING THE BOOK

The time had come for God to select a new king of Israel. He sent his prophet Samuel to meet a man named Jesse who had eight sons. Samuel looked at Jesse's oldest son who was tall and good-looking. He thought, "This has got to be the guy to be the next king." But God said, "No." So Samuel looked at the next six sons, but God didn't choose any of them. Finally Samuel asked Jesse if he had any other sons. Jesse said that he had one more, the youngest, but that he was out taking care of the sheep. They sent for him and a little later, in walked a young boy named David. Much to everyone's surprise, God told Samuel that he was to be the next king of Israel.

Read 1 Samuel 16:1-13. Notice especially verse 7: "Man looks at the outward appearance, but the LORD looks at the heart." What did Samuel learn that day?

_____

_____

_____

_____

_____

LESSONS LEARNED

What do you think God is trying to tell you from today's Scripture? How often do you find yourself making statements about people based totally on their physical appearances?

_____

_____

_____

_____

_____

_____

_____

_____

TODAY'S ASSIGNMENT

How can you apply this lesson today? Maybe you need to look at some people in a new way.

_____

_____

_____

_____

_____

_____

_____

_____

_____

TALKING TO GOD

Take a few minutes to ask God to help you live this out through the day. What do you need to say to him today?

_____

_____

_____

_____

_____

_____

_____

_____

_____

_____

OTHER THOUGHTS

_____

_____

_____

_____

_____

_____

_____

_____

_____

_____

_____

DAY 3 | PICTURES OF FRIENDS
God never fails

A locker door is a great place to post pictures of friends. These pictures remind you of fun times and friendships. Every time you open your locker, you're greeted with smiling faces that remind you of great experiences.

Pictures of friends are wonderful, but unfortunately the pictures sometimes last longer than the friendships. Everyone has gotten into an argument with a good friend. Everyone has experienced the pain that comes from being angry with a friend. Most people can even relate to what it feels like to be betrayed by a close friend. In the real world, friendships change and sometimes end altogether.

Stephen and Blake were best friends—they played on the baseball team, lived in the same neighborhood and had the same class schedule. They were practically inseparable, until one day while they were playing catch, Blake accidentally threw a baseball through a window of Stephen's neighbors' house. Since the neighbors weren't home, Blake made Stephen promise not to tell anyone that he had broken the window; then he headed home.

That evening the neighbor came over and talked to Stephen's dad about the window. Since the boys often played catch with a baseball in the yard, they were obvious suspects. Stephen admitted to playing catch and confessed that he had failed to catch the ball that Blake had thrown. The neighbor was glad that Stephen had told the truth and asked Stephen to pay to replace the window.

When Blake found out what had happened, he was mad that Stephen had "ratted" on him. Stephen asked Blake to pay for half of the window since he had thrown the ball, but Blake refused. Neither of them could resolve the problem and that virtually ended their friendship. They avoided each other at school, didn't hang out anymore and practically stopped speaking to each other altogether.

Friends will come and go. You'll make many new friends and lose others. It is a rare friend that sticks with you throughout your whole life. So when your friends fail you, where can you turn?

HITTING THE BOOK

Even though friends sometimes let you down, God makes some great promises that he'll never break. In Joshua 1:9 he promises, "Have I not commanded you? Be strong and courageous. Do not be terrified; do not be discouraged, for the LORD your God will be with you wherever you go." There is one friend who will never fail you. Proverbs 18:24 says, "Friends come and friends go, but a true friend sticks by you like family" (*Message*). What do these words mean to you?

_____

_____

_____

_____

_____

_____

_____

_____

_____

_____

_____

LESSONS LEARNED

What do you think God is trying to tell you from his Word today?
Do you have a relationship with a friend that needs to be repaired?
Who is it?

_____

_____

_____

_____

_____

_____

_____

_____

_____

_____

TODAY'S ASSIGNMENT

How can you apply this lesson today?

_____

_____

_____

_____

_____

_____

_____

_____

_____

TALKING TO GOD

Ask God to help you live this out through the day. What do you need to
say to him today?

_____

_____

_____

_____

_____

_____

_____

_____

_____

_____

OTHER THOUGHTS

_____

_____

_____

_____

_____

_____

_____

_____

_____

DAY 4 | COAT
God protects you

I don't know if it was the neighborhood that I grew up in or what, but some of the people at my bus stop were really strange. One guy in particular, Jason, was always doing unusual things. He would eat dirty snow that he had scraped off the road and tell us it was a salty snow cone. He often crossed the street to the bus stop as slowly as possible, making morning drivers more than a bit frustrated.

One winter Jason really outdid himself. He decided that he was not going to wear a coat at all that winter. We lived in the northern part of the United States, and it gets pretty cold there. It wasn't that Jason didn't have a coat—in fact, he had a nice one. But Jason was determined—for whatever reason—to withstand the cold winter without a coat.

As it got cooler, the rest of my classmates and I would wear jackets or sweaters. Not Jason. He'd come to the bus stop wearing only his shirt. As winter set in, the rest of us would stand there trying to keep warm, wearing our heavy coats and gloves; Jason would walk slowly across the street wearing only a shirt. He'd cross his arms and stomp his feet to try to keep warm, but he was fighting a losing battle. As the days got colder, Jason's lips got bluer and bluer. It finally got to the point that he couldn't take it anymore, and he had to wear a coat to the bus stop. We all laughed at Jason, and none of us could under-stand why it had taken him so long to give in and wear his coat.

Jason thought that he could withstand winter's cruel blast wearing only a thin shirt. He was wrong. Jason needed his coat for protec-tion from the cold, the rain and the wind. When it gets cold out-side, most people wear coats to protect themselves. When we get to school, we put our coats in our lockers for the day, unless we have classes in multiple buildings.

We wear a variety of coats, each with its own specific purpose. A dress coat is worn on special occasions such as going to church, a wedding, a funeral or on a fancy date. A raincoat or poncho protects us from wind and rain while watching a ball game, walking in the rain, camping or going to an outdoor concert. Athletic jackets help our bodies stay warm after stretching out during practice or while playing in a game. A windbreaker is lightweight, but it can keep the wind away on cool evenings.

Coats are important. Even though we may buy them based mostly on style, their ultimate purpose is to protect us from the elements. On a bitterly cold freezing morning, be thankful for the warmth your coat gives you.

Sometimes in life you need protection. You need a shield against harsh situations. God offers you that protection.

HITTING THE BOOK

Psalm 18:2 says, "The LORD is my rock, my fortress and my deliverer; my God is my rock, in whom I take refuge. He is my shield and the horn of my salvation, my stronghold."

Has God protected or delivered you from anything lately? What was it?

_____

_____

_____

_____

LESSONS LEARNED

What do you think God is trying to tell you through his Word today?

_____
_____
_____
_____
_____
_____
_____
_____
_____

TODAY'S ASSIGNMENT

How can you apply this lesson today?

_____
_____
_____
_____
_____
_____
_____
_____
_____

TALKING TO GOD

Take a few minutes to ask God to help you carry this lesson with you throughout the day. What do you need to say to him today?

_____

_____

_____

_____

_____

_____

_____

_____

_____

OTHER THOUGHTS

_____

_____

_____

_____

_____

_____

_____

_____

_____

_____

DAY 5 | CANDY
God satisfies you

I love candy! I love chocolate! I love chocolate candy! That's why Halloween has always been one of my favorite holidays—I was continually amazed that on October 31, people would just hand out free candy! When I got home from trick-or-treating, my parents would always check out the candy to make sure that it was OK—no matter how old I was. Then they'd warn me not to eat too much of it at one time because they knew that candy was a weakness for me. Usually, I couldn't help myself. Within a week my candy was gone, and I was trying to get more from my brother and sister.

My candy cravings didn't miraculously end when all of the Halloween candy was gone either. I struggled with that temptation often. When I was in band, we had to raise money for new uniforms. Our band director decided that we would raise the money by selling candy. So we sold boxes of candy to students, teachers, parents, neighbors and anyone else who would buy it. I thought that my love for candy would make me an excellent salesman, but I wasn't totally accurate.

The day they gave us the candy to sell, I put forty-eight boxes in my locker. We were to sell them for one dollar per box and then turn the money in to our band director at the end of the week. I remember thinking all day long about having that candy in my locker. On the way home, I put three dollars in my money box and ate three boxes of candy. After dinner that night, I bought and ate three more boxes. The next day at school, I sold a few boxes and ate several more. By the end of the week, I was out of candy—I had sold twenty boxes and eaten twenty-eight—and feeling a bit sick to my stomach.

Most of us have had candy in our lockers at one time or another. Maybe you've sold it to raise money, or maybe you keep some stashed in your locker for when you need a sugar rush. Either way, almost everyone loves candy. It's a fun snack—eaten in moderation—but if you eat a ton of it, you'll get sick.

Life is filled with good things that are meant to be enjoyed in moderation. But when the pursuit of pleasure takes control of our lives, problems arise. It doesn't matter what the gratification is. It might be something as simple as eating candy or watching TV, or it might be as harmful as alcohol or drugs. When these "pleasures" are taken to the extreme, we can get into trouble quickly.

HITTING THE BOOK

Psalm 107:8, 9 says, "Let them give thanks to the LORD for his unfailing love and his wonderful deeds for men, for he satisfies the thirsty and fills the hungry with good things."

What do you think God is trying to tell you today?

LESSONS LEARNED

What is one "pleasure" that is beginning to take control of you in an unhealthy way?

_____

_____

_____

_____

_____

_____

_____

_____

_____

_____

How can you stop this?

_____

_____

_____

_____

_____

_____

_____

_____

_____

How can you let God satisfy your hunger?

_____
_____
_____
_____
_____
_____
_____
_____
_____
_____

TODAY'S ASSIGNMENT
How can you apply this lesson today?

_____
_____
_____
_____
_____
_____
_____
_____
_____
_____

Think of one activity that is taking up too much time in your life. Write a pledge here to limit this activity this week.

_____

_____

_____

_____

_____

_____

_____

_____

Think of one spiritual activity you need to spend more time doing. Write a promise to yourself to do that.

_____

_____

_____

_____

_____

_____

_____

_____

_____

_____

TALKING TO GOD

Take some time to pray and ask God to help you remember today's lesson and carry it with you throughout the day.

_____

_____

_____

_____

_____

_____

_____

_____

_____

OTHER THOUGHTS

_____

_____

_____

_____

_____

_____

_____

_____

_____

_____

DAY 6 | TENNIS SHOES
Run the race well

Do you remember your first pair of really good tennis shoes? Maybe they were Nike®, Reebok®, New Balance® or some other brand. Did you have to listen to a speech from your parents about how they never paid that much for a pair of shoes and then promise that if they bought them for you, you'd never ask for another thing for the rest of your life?

I remember a conversation like that as if it were yesterday. My first pair of good tennis shoes was a pair of blue Adidas®. It seemed as though everyone in my school was wearing them—except me. I begged and begged my parents for weeks, and finally on my birthday, I got them. I promised that I would take care of them forever. I can remember wearing them to school that first time. I was so proud. I avoided mud puddles and did my best to keep them looking new.

I loved my tennis shoes. I wore them everywhere—PE class, school, around the house, at the gym, to soccer practice—they were the best shoes. They were so versatile that I could do almost anything while wearing them. When I wore them, I felt that I was a better athlete because I could run faster and jump higher. They were great!

Many students are involved in some sort of athletic competition. It might be basketball, baseball, soccer, volleyball, cheerleading, swimming, gymnastics, karate or football. The list goes on and on. Almost every sport has its own type of shoes. Having the right shoe for your sport makes a difference in the way you practice, play and perform. And whether you realize it or not, if you're a Christian, you're in a competition—a race—and you need to be sure that you've got the right shoes on.

Every follower of Jesus is out there every day competing to do the right thing and facing the challenges of the opposition. It is a daily challenge, but each day we can get stronger. Each day we can get a little better at standing up to the competition of our enemy.

HITTING THE BOOK

Here's what the Bible says about being in a spiritual race. First Corinthians 9:24, 25 states, "Remember that in a race everyone runs, but only one person gets the prize. You also must run in such a way that you will win. All athletes practice strict self-control. They do it to win a prize that will fade away, but we do it for an eternal prize" (NLT).

We need to remember that we are competing to get a crown. That crown is eternal life in Heaven. It is a prize that will never get dusty, lost or be forgotten—it's eternal! How well are you running and competing for God?

_____

_____

_____

_____

_____

_____

_____

_____

_____

LESSONS LEARNED

What do you think God is trying to tell you today? What do you think you have to do to "run in such a way that you will win"?

_____

_____

_____

_____

_____

_____

_____

_____

_____

_____

_____

What obstacles make it hard for you to run this race for God well?

_____

_____

_____

_____

_____

_____

_____

_____

_____

_____

_____

Who or what are you competing against? Do you have a strategy for beating your opposition? What is it?

What do you have to do to become a stronger runner?

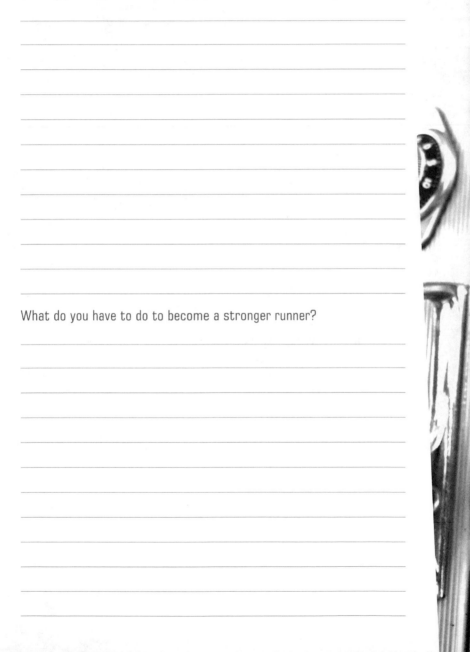

TODAY'S ASSIGNMENT

How can you apply the lesson today?

_____

_____

_____

_____

_____

_____

_____

_____

_____

_____

_____

Name three ways you can practice self-control today.

_____

_____

_____

_____

_____

_____

_____

_____

_____

TALKING TO GOD

Take a few minutes to ask God to help you carry this lesson with you throughout the day. What do you need to say to him today?

_____

_____

_____

_____

_____

_____

_____

_____

OTHER THOUGHTS

_____

_____

_____

_____

_____

_____

_____

DAY 7 | MUSICAL INSTRUMENT
You have a talent

I remember setting the alarm on my watch to go off at 2:33 P.M. each day. The bell rang at 2:38 P.M. to dismiss everyone from school. Since I was in the band, I was allowed to leave class five minutes early to get my instrument from my locker so I wouldn't miss the bus. Whether I intended to practice or not, I took my instrument home every day, just so that I could leave class five minutes early. But my love for band wasn't based solely on the early dismissal.

I grew up in a musical family—everyone played one instrument or another. Since I was the only guy who played clarinet, I decided early on to avoid ridicule by being really good at it. So I practiced and practiced, and by the time I got to junior high, I was first chair! For most of my junior and senior high years, I stayed in that position. I learned that if I wanted to be the best at something like playing an instrument, it would take a lot of practice and hard work.

I'll never forget going to a state band competition in high school. Four of us got together to make a woodwind quartet. We practiced our piece of music every day during band. As the state competition grew closer, we added some after-school practices. The piece of music that we were performing was difficult and long, so it took a long time to memorize it, but we finally got to the point that we could almost play it in our sleep. We were anticipating placing first in the competition.

Then the week before the competition, Angie, one of our quartet members, broke her finger playing volleyball. She had her finger put in a cast and couldn't play her flute for a month. There was no way that she would be able to compete, and we had only seven days to go! To be honest, the rest of us panicked a little. We finally decided that instead of quitting the competition after working so hard, we'd bring in another flute player, named Tisha. She wasn't quite as good as Angie, but she was our best option. She worked diligently to memorize the piece and blend with the rest of the quartet.

Finally, the day of the competition arrived. We played pretty well, but we knew that we hadn't done as well as we would have if Angie had played with us. We took third place. Considering the last-minute substitution, we weren't too disappointed, because we knew we had done our best with what we had been given.

HITTING THE BOOK

God has given every person gifts and talents. It is up to each individual to use them to the best of his or her ability. Maybe your gift is music, making friends, speaking in front of crowds, playing sports or inventing new ways of doing things. Whatever it is, it is up to you to use that God-given talent to the best of your ability. God has uniquely gifted you. Don't try to be someone else!

Read Romans 12:4-10. What gifts, abilities or talents has God given you?

_____

_____

_____

_____

_____

_____

_____

_____

LESSONS LEARNED

What do you think God is trying to tell you through his Word today?

_____

_____

_____

_____

_____

_____

_____

_____

_____

_____

TODAY'S ASSIGNMENT

How can you use your gifts and talents today?

_____

_____

_____

_____

_____

_____

_____

_____

_____

TALKING TO GOD

Ask God to help you live this out through the day. What do you need to say to him today?

_____

_____

_____

_____

_____

_____

_____

_____

_____

_____

OTHER THOUGHTS

_____

_____

_____

_____

_____

_____

_____

_____

_____

DAY 8 | LOCK

God knows your sins but still loves you

Every locker has a lock on the outside to keep the items inside secure. (That's why they're called "lockers.") Depending on your school, and unless you were lucky enough to have key locks, you either had to bring your own combination lock to school or you were given the combination of the one built into the door.

I remember being given the combination to my new locker on the first day of school. I looked at the three numbers and tried to memorize them. Fourteen to the right, twenty-two to the left, seventeen to the right and pull the lock open. It all seems so simple now. But the first few days of school, everyone concentrated on learning that combination, so they wouldn't have to pull out the written combinations each time they wanted to get into their lockers.

That lock provided security for my locker. It kept me from worrying that someone might get into my locker and steal some of my stuff or put something in my locker that didn't belong there. The contents of my locker would remain totally anonymous as long as I didn't reveal the combination to anyone.

I'll never forget sitting in class one day and hearing a loud commotion out in the hallway. Suddenly several police officers and a police dog rushed past the door. No one in the class knew what was going on, but it didn't take long for the story to get around school. Evidently a boy named Mike shared a locker with several of his friends. When Mike started keeping marijuana in his locker, one of his friends found it and reported it to the assistant principal. The assistant principal called the police, who brought in a drug-sniffing dog. They cut the lock off of Mike's locker, and the dog found the drugs.

Mike had tried to keep a secret hidden in his locker. He thought that his secret was safe, but it wasn't. Mike's friend cared about him too much to let him get messed up with drugs. His friend did the right thing.

Maybe you have secret sins locked deep inside. You may keep them locked away and never let anyone inside to see them. You may feel as though they are too bad to get help, and even think thoughts like, *How could God love me? I'm too bad!*

But believe it or not, just the opposite is true. God already knows all the bad stuff about you, and he still loves you. He wants you to come clean. He wants to help. He wants what is best for his children. He doesn't want you to keep hiding your secret sins in the locker of your heart.

HITTING THE BOOK

First John 3:19, 20 says, "It is by our actions that we know we are living in the truth, so we will be confident when we stand before the LORD, even if our hearts condemn us. For God is greater than our hearts, and he knows everything" (*NLT*).

What secret sin do you have locked away? Why not confess it to God right now?

_____

_____

_____

_____

_____

_____

_____

LESSONS LEARNED

What do you think God is trying to tell you today?

_____

_____

_____

_____

_____

_____

_____

_____

_____

_____

TODAY'S ASSIGNMENT

How can you apply this lesson today?

_____

_____

_____

_____

_____

_____

_____

_____

_____

TALKING TO GOD

Take some time to ask God to help you deal with this truth today. What do you need to say to him?

_____

_____

_____

_____

_____

_____

_____

_____

_____

_____

_____

OTHER THOUGHTS

_____

_____

_____

_____

_____

_____

_____

_____

_____

DAY 9 | SOFT DRINK
Only God can refresh you

'll never forget the summer that I decided that it was time to get a job so that I'd finally have my own money to spend. My first real paying job was cutting grass for older people in my neighborhood. Sometimes the pay wasn't that great, but they almost always had homemade cookies waiting for me when I finished the job. My favorite customer that summer was Mrs. Bernadine, an elderly, retired kindergarten teacher. Her yard wasn't that big, but it was filled with beautiful flowers and plants. She took great pride in the way her lawn looked.

It usually didn't take too long to mow Mrs. Bernadine's grass—as long as her lawn mower started. She had a really old lawn mower that often needed a little coaxing to get it started. Sometimes it would start on the first pull and other times it would take twenty or thirty pulls and some tinkering to get the old engine to run. I might have to clean off the spark plug or clean out the dead grass from underneath the mower to get it working properly. Mrs. Bernadine really needed a new mower, but because she lived on a fixed income she didn't have the money for one. So each week we'd work together to get the mower running, and then I'd do my best to cut the whole yard before the mower died.

After I had finished cutting her grass and put the lawn mower back in her shed, she'd come out to pay me. Every week she'd give me the money, but that's not all she'd do. Mrs. Bernadine would also bring out a can of ice-cold Coke®. She'd always say, "It's so hot out here. You need something to cool you off." My mouth would start to water as I saw the drops of condensation dripping off the can. That first drink seemed to cool my entire body from the inside out. It was, without a doubt, the best tasting Coke® I would have all week long.

It got to the point where I'd be cutting Mrs. Bernadine's grass under the hot sun, nearly sweating to death and wanting to quit—but the thought of that ice-cold Coke® kept me going. I knew that no matter how hot I got, there would be a soft drink waiting for me at the end to help cool me off.

Unfortunately, overcoming all of life's challenges isn't quite as easy as opening a can of Coke®. If it were, our lockers would be filled with cans of pop—one for each assignment we turned in and for every exam we took. But there is something that can give us comfort and refreshment no matter how difficult the challenges we face are. One day Jesus met a woman who had a ton of problems in her life. She had no friends. She had been divorced five times and was living with yet another guy. Life for her was not very good. In the midst of all this, Jesus asked her for a drink of water. Then he offered her a drink that would quench her thirst forever. She was intrigued and asked to learn more about this water.

HITTING THE BOOK

Scientists calculate that the human body cannot last longer than three days without drinking water. When Jesus was talking to the woman at the well, he was talking about water that would satisfy thirst forever. Take a few minutes to read about this amazing water that Jesus offered the woman in John 4:1-30.

_____

_____

_____

_____

_____

LESSONS LEARNED

Have you ever needed God's comfort and refreshment?

_____

_____

_____

_____

_____

_____

_____

_____

_____

_____

When? What happened?

_____

_____

_____

_____

_____

_____

_____

_____

_____

_____

_____

What do you think God is trying to tell you about quenching your thirst today?

_____

_____

_____

_____

_____

_____

_____

_____

_____

TODAY'S ASSIGNMENT
How can you apply this teaching today?

_____

_____

_____

_____

_____

_____

_____

_____

_____

_____

_____

Maybe you need to offer someone else a chance to drink "living water."
How could you do that today?

_____

_____

_____

_____

_____

_____

_____

_____

_____

_____

_____

TALKING TO GOD

Ask God to help you thirst for his presence today. What do you need to
say to him?

_____

_____

_____

_____

_____

_____

OTHER THOUGHTS

DAY 10 | STICKERS
Put Jesus first

One of the best things about having your own locker is being free to decorate however you want. One of the ways that I showed my likes and interests was by collecting stickers on the inside of my locker. I put up bumper stickers with my favorite sayings. I posted stickers from my favorite bands and radio stations. I tried to cover the entire inside of my locker door with stickers.

The stickers did more than just look good, they made a statement about who I was. Anyone who opened my locker would know my favorite things. I had stickers promoting the St. Louis Cardinals baseball team, the local rock station K-SHE 95, my favorite bands, REO Speedwagon, Journey and Rush. I also had a sticker with my graduation year on it, because I was looking forward to it so much.

I was always careful about which stickers I put up in my locker—these stickers represented important things in my life. But one day I realized that even though I was a Christian, there weren't any stickers in my locker that made that obvious. I was perplexed by the fact that God was missing from the stickers that represented things that I liked and that were a part of my life.

I knew that if I put a "religious" sticker in my locker, my friends would see it. If they saw it, they might make assumptions about me. *What if they didn't like me anymore? What if they made fun of me? What if they asked me questions? What if I didn't know the answers? What if . . . ? What if . . . ?*

It took me a couple of weeks to decide that I really wanted God to be part of every aspect of my life—even my locker. So I bought a sticker that said, "I love Jesus!" and put it up in my locker. I admit that I was a little nervous about it at first, but then I felt great about my decision. I can remember many days when I was having a rough time or facing an extremely tough test that I looked to that sticker and was reminded that not only did I love Jesus, but he also loved me.

To my surprise, only one person commented on that sticker the entire year. It was a girl who was also a Christian. She said she liked it, and asked where she could get one for her locker. I didn't lose any friends because I put a Jesus sticker in my locker, and I was glad to know for sure that I'm not ashamed that Jesus is part of my life.

HITTING THE BOOK

Read Matthew 16:13-19. There were many people in the Bible who took a stand for God. One of the most famous was Peter. One time Jesus and his disciples were in the area of Caesarea Philippi. This area was filled with false religions. History tells us that there was a pagan shrine there to honor Pan, the Greek and Roman god of nature.

In the midst of all this opposition and false religion, Jesus asked his disciples who people thought he was. They gave him several answers. Then he asked, "Who do you say I am?" Peter gave a classic answer that was much more than just a simple identification. Peter's statement was not only the right answer, but it has become what is known as the "good confession." Peter didn't care who heard his answer, or what they thought about him. He was saying that he believed that Jesus was number one, above anyone or anything else in his life. What do you think about this?

Who do you say Jesus is?

_____

_____

_____

_____

_____

_____

_____

_____

_____

LESSONS LEARNED

What do you think God is trying to tell you today? Can people see that you are a Christian? How?

_____

_____

_____

_____

_____

_____

_____

_____

_____

TODAY'S ASSIGNMENT

What are some practical ways you can live for Jesus today?

_____

_____

_____

_____

_____

_____

_____

_____

_____

_____

What is one way you need to take a stand for God today?

_____

_____

_____

_____

_____

_____

_____

_____

_____

_____

_____

Write here what you would say if someone asked you "Who is Jesus?" Think about some people who might need to hear this answer.

_____

_____

_____

_____

_____

_____

_____

_____

_____

_____

_____

_____

_____

_____

_____

TALKING TO GOD

Take some time to ask God to give you the courage to live for him today. What do you need to say to him?

_____

_____

_____

_____

_____

OTHER THOUGHTS

DAY 11 | PAPER
Your life is a letter

We've all been there. It's your first day back to school after summer vacation. You walk into class and sit down. The bell rings. The teacher introduces himself and then instructs everyone to take out a blank piece of paper and something to write with. Instantly, fear seizes everyone in the classroom. As each person reaches down to get a piece of paper he glances at his neighbor and exchanges an unsure look that says, *What's coming next?*

Quickly, people think they might be in for a pop quiz. But on the first day of the year, it would have to be a review of what students remembered from the year before. The teacher probably wouldn't count it for the overall grade, right? Or what if it were an essay test? What if this teacher is a ruthless person who loves to torture students on a frequent basis? What will you do? How will you survive?

Suddenly, you come to your senses. Even though you are sweating over the thought of a pop quiz or essay test, you begin to think about the situation. *This is just the beginning of the school year. Most teachers don't start out by humiliating their students on the first day of school.* And then the teacher steps forward and instructs you to write an essay about what you did during summer break. *Whew!* Everyone lets out a sigh and a sense of relief pervades the room.

You begin to write an essay that chronicles the events of your summer break. You write about your family's vacation, a trip you took with the church youth group, staying up late at night and sleeping in until the crack of noon. You lose yourself in writing about everything that you did during your summer vacation.

Once you become a Christian, your life becomes like a clean sheet of paper. There is no story written on it, but you begin to write your story by the life that you lead. We all want the essays of our lives to be good, but honestly, there are chapters in all of our stories that we're not proud of. But no matter whether good or bad, our life stories are written by the actions we choose to take.

HITTING THE BOOK

Read 2 Corinthians 3:1-3. The apostle Paul wrote these words. It was customary for people who traveled to carry with them a letter from their home church that vouched for them. It said something like: "This guy is a good guy. He is trustworthy; listen to his message." Paul broke that tradition by saying that we didn't need a letter of recommendation, but that our lives should speak for themselves.

The letter that you carry with you is not made from ink and paper. This letter is based on the actions of your life. Your actions are open for others to see. They tell a story about your love for God and your commitment to him.

What kind of letter do your actions write? When other people read the letter of your life, what does it say about you? What does it say about your relationship with God?

_____

_____

_____

_____

_____

LESSONS LEARNED

What do you think God is trying to tell you today?

_____

_____

_____

_____

_____

_____

_____

_____

_____

_____

TODAY'S ASSIGNMENT

How can you apply this teaching today?

_____

_____

_____

_____

_____

_____

_____

_____

_____

TALKING TO GOD

Take a few minutes to ask God to help you carry this lesson with you throughout the day. What do you need to say to him today?

_____

_____

_____

_____

_____

_____

_____

_____

_____

_____

_____

OTHER THOUGHTS

_____

_____

_____

_____

_____

_____

_____

_____

_____

DAY 12 | TRASH
God forgives your sins

D an was always an odd kid. He never really understood the importance of personal hygiene. The fact is, he often looked dirty and had a very unusual odor about him, so his classmates tagged him with the nickname, "Pigpen."

Dan's locker was the dirtiest, most cluttered locker in school. Several times a year the assistant principal would bring Dan to his locker and have him take out all of the trash, wadded-up papers, candy wrappers and soft drink cans and throw them into a large garbage can. Dan would stand next to the assistant principal with his head down, not looking at anyone. Then he would slowly clean out all the trash in his locker.

An amazing thing would happen when Dan had finished cleaning the trash out of his locker. While most students would be devastated after having been humiliated in front of the whole school, Dan wasn't. He seemed to take pride in the fact that his locker was spotless. He would even brag about having the cleanest locker in school. He was proud that his locker was neat and clean.

Dan's pride didn't last very long. For some reason he couldn't keep his locker clean. Soon it would be cluttered with more old school papers, snack wrappers, drink cans and anything else that found its way to the bottom of his locker. It wouldn't be too long before it was impossible to tell that Dan had ever cleaned out his locker at all!

Sometimes our lives are like Dan's locker— cluttered and dirty with mistakes we have made and wrong things we've done. Our lives get filled with bad stuff—sin. Sometimes we need someone else to help us clean up our lives. We may not even realize how bad things are until someone loves us enough to confront us on all the garbage we're stashing in our lives. Often we justify our garbage by comparing ourselves to others who appear to have more junk than we do.

But just like Dan, when we come clean before God, we feel great. We feel as though a burden has been lifted off our backs. When we follow Christ, we have confidence that God forgives our sins. The problem is that just like Dan's locker, we may begin again to clutter our lives with the same bad things, mistakes and sins.

The key that Dan either didn't understand or refused to follow is this: if you clean out your locker a little bit every day, it stays clean. The same concept is true in our lives. If we have a relationship with God in which we confess our sins to him daily, he'll forgive them and get rid of them immediately.

HITTING THE BOOK

First John 1:8, 9 promises, "If we say we have no sin, we are only fooling ourselves and refusing to accept the truth. But if we confess our sins to him, he is faithful and just to forgive us and to cleanse us from every wrong" (NLT). These verses say it pretty clearly. Just like Dan needed to clean the trash out of his locker each day, you need to confess your sins to God every day so that he will forgive you.

Take some time to think about *your* trash. What sins do you struggle with the most?

_____

_____

_____

_____

LESSONS LEARNED

What do you think the gentle voice of God is speaking from his Word today?

_____

_____

_____

_____

_____

_____

_____

_____

_____

_____

TODAY'S ASSIGNMENT

How can you apply this to your life today?

_____

_____

_____

_____

_____

_____

_____

_____

_____

TALKING TO GOD

Ask God to help you deal with this today. What do you need to say to him?

_____

_____

_____

_____

_____

_____

_____

_____

_____

_____

OTHER THOUGHTS

_____

_____

_____

_____

_____

_____

_____

_____

_____

DAY 13 | NOTES
Encourage others

I'm willing to bet that students have been passing notes since the time they were lumped together in the first classroom. For some reason we just can't always wait for an opportunity to talk to our friends—the information we have is just *too important* to keep to ourselves any longer! Even though most notes don't really say much, getting a note from a friend can be the highlight of your day—the message was specifically written for and delivered to you. A note can deepen a friendship, share details about what's going on at school or make you feel like you're in the loop.

Sometimes notes are printed on cool paper or folded in an elaborate origami design that includes instructions for opening. But no matter how the note is presented, the most important thing about a note is what is written on the inside. Notes definitely vary in subject and depth of content. They range from "I like you. Do you like me? Circle *yes* or *no*" to eloquent confessions of love. It can be comforting to read a note that begins with a familiar phrase from a good friend. Unless a boyfriend or girlfriend is dumping you via the note, most of the time the news is good, and you're glad to be reading it.

I had a tendency to stash the notes I received in my locker so that I could look back at them whenever I needed. Now I keep a file that's called Encouragement in one of my desk drawers. It's filled with all the notes of encouragement that I have received from people. When I'm having a down day, I look through that file, reread the notes, and feel better because I'm reminded of how much people care about me.

Christians sometimes need to be encouraged. We also need to encourage others. Why not write a note of encouragement to someone you care about and help lift her up? You never know when you'll need a little support in return.

HITTING THE BOOK

If we are all on God's team, we should encourage each other. Hebrews 10:24, 25 challenges us with these words: "Let's see how inventive we can be in encouraging love and helping out, not avoiding worshiping together as some do but spurring each other on, especially as we see the big Day approaching" (*Message*).

What do these words bring to your mind?

_____

_____

_____

_____

_____

_____

_____

What does it mean to you to encourage love and help out?

_____

_____

_____

_____

_____

_____

_____

_____

LESSONS LEARNED

Who is someone that has encouraged you lately?

What did he or she say or do?

Who is someone you need to encourage?

_____

_____

_____

_____

_____

_____

_____

_____

_____

How can you do it?

_____

_____

_____

_____

_____

_____

_____

_____

_____

_____

TODAY'S ASSIGNMENT

How can you be an encourager today?

_____

_____

_____

_____

_____

_____

_____

_____

_____

Write here some inventive ways you have seen others encouraging people or helping out this week.

_____

_____

_____

_____

_____

_____

_____

_____

_____

_____

TALKING TO GOD

Ask God to give you opportunities to encourage others today.

OTHER THOUGHTS

DAY 14 | BACKPACK
God will carry your load

Backpacks are great inventions. They allow you to carry your books, homework, pens and pencils, keys, student planner, lunch and anything else you need without having to wrestle with them in your arms. You simply put your stuff in your backpack, strap it on and forget about it until you need something out of it. But backpacks are just like everything else—if you don't use them properly, they'll eventually cause problems.

By the time you load your backpack up with books and other necessities, it can weigh a lot! Most of us only have to carry the books and other supplies we need for a couple of classes at a time. But students in Lee County, Florida, have to carry *all* of their school supplies with them every day, because the school board had the lockers removed from the county's schools. Now some students are complaining about the weight of their backpacks.

The school district took a survey and determined that the average loaded backpack weighs 18 pounds. Students, parents and even some doctors are concerned that serious back problems will develop from students having to carry around that much weight. One principal said that he knows of a 60-pound sixth-grade girl whose backpack weighs 17 pounds. That's almost 30 percent of her entire body weight riding on her back every day.

Carrying a load like that on our backs can wear us down. But many of us carry much heavier burdens that aren't in our backpacks. We carry around loads of guilt, fear, shame, apprehension, sorrow and sadness. Even though we can't physically see the loads we carry, these weights drag us down. They affect every part of our lives—our attitudes, friendships, grades and relationships with our parents, just to name a few.

Maybe you are carrying a load that is more than just the weight in your backpack. Maybe you have done something wrong and worry about people finding out. Maybe you and your family are going through something really major and you think about it constantly. Maybe someone you care about has hurt you deeply. You carry the pain with you every day. You think about it constantly. Whatever it is, most of us are carrying around an extra burden.

God doesn't want you to carry your problems around by yourself. He sent Jesus to help lighten your load. Just think—the God of the universe sent his one-and-only Son to earth because he loves you. Wow! What a concept! God wants to take your load off your back. He wants to help carry it. He wants you to rest in him like you do when you go to sleep at the end of a long day.

HITTING THE BOOK

Jesus says in Matthew 11:28-30, "Come to me, all of you who are weary and carry heavy burdens, and I will give you rest. Take my yoke upon you. Let me teach you, because I am humble and gentle, and you will find rest for your souls. For my yoke fits perfectly, and the burden I give you is light" (*NLT*).

Jesus invites all who are tired of carrying around heavy emotional loads to come to him. He wants to provide perfect rest. He wants to help carry your burdens. How do these words make you feel?

_____

_____

_____

_____

LESSONS LEARNED

What are you carrying that you need to give over to Jesus?

_____

_____

_____

_____

_____

_____

_____

_____

_____

_____

How can you begin to do that?

_____

_____

_____

_____

_____

_____

_____

_____

_____

_____

What would it mean for you to find rest for your soul?

_____

_____

_____

_____

_____

_____

_____

_____

_____

_____

What do you think Jesus has to teach you today?

_____

_____

_____

_____

_____

_____

_____

_____

_____

_____

_____

_____

TODAY'S ASSIGNMENT

How can you allow Jesus to help carry your burdens today?

_____

_____

_____

_____

_____

_____

_____

_____

_____

_____

Once you give your burden over to Jesus, write here how you feel.

_____

_____

_____

_____

_____

_____

_____

_____

_____

TALKING TO GOD

Take a few minutes to ask God to help you live this out through the
day. What do you need to say to him today?

_____

_____

_____

_____

_____

_____

_____

_____

_____

OTHER THOUGHTS

_____

_____

_____

_____

_____

_____

_____

_____

_____

_____

DAY 15 | AIR FRESHENER
Don't be a hypocrite

After a few months of forgotten lunches, misguided science projects, smelly soccer shoes and moldy gym clothes, a locker may become the habitat for a new life—form and produce some pretty nasty odors. It's amazing how the small space of a locker can accumulate such a plethora of odors.

A friend of mine had a locker that always smelled really good. This intrigued me because some days my locker smelled so bad that one whiff would make my eyes water and the stuff in his locker didn't look all that different from mine. So one day I asked him what his secret was. He looked at me like I was asking a silly question but then pulled out a vanilla-scented air freshener that was shaped like a Christmas tree. What a great idea! I mean, we had air fresheners all over our house, but I had never thought to use one in my locker.

After school that day I went out and bought an air freshener for my locker. No matter what nasty stuff was growing in there, the vanilla aroma covered it up. But eventually I had to really clean out my locker because no amount of potent air fresheners could cover up what was going on in there. Our lives are kind of like our lockers in that respect—we can only cover up the nasty stuff for so long until we just can't hide it anymore.

I went to school with a guy named Patrick. He was the president of his youth group, the student leader of our Fellowship of Christian Athletes and the co-founder of the S.A.D.D. (Students Against Drunk Driving) chapter at our school. Everyone looked up to him. We thought that he was a great guy who really had his life together.

The problem was that all these things were just a front, and eventually the ugly truth came out at our senior prom. Patrick had gone out with some of his friends and gotten drunk. When he finally arrived at the prom, he was totally wasted. He thought no one would notice or care, but it was obvious that he was a hypocrite, and we had bought into the lie. He hurt a lot of people and lost out on a number of opportunities because of the poor choices he made.

Some of us use a lot of air freshener—we may act really good in front of our parents, youth pastors, teachers and coaches, but our "secret" lives are the total opposite. We may think that the good things we do will cover up the bad things but, as with real air fresheners, eventually we lose the ability to smell good. The bad stuff comes to the surface. We can't hide our sins forever—and we can never hide them from God.

HITTING THE BOOK

Read Luke 6:39-45. Some people are really good at pointing out flaws in other people. The problem is that they often neglect to see their own issues. God tells us that we need to take care of our own sins before we try to help others.

What speck needs your attention? How will you try to handle the problem?

_____

_____

_____

_____

_____

_____

LESSONS LEARNED

What do you think God is trying to tell you through his Word today?

TODAY'S ASSIGNMENT

How can you apply this lesson about hypocrisy today?

TALKING TO GOD

Take a few minutes to ask God to help you carry this lesson with you throughout the day. What do you need to say to him?

_____

_____

_____

_____

_____

_____

_____

_____

_____

_____

OTHER THOUGHTS

_____

_____

_____

_____

_____

_____

_____

_____

_____

_____

DAY 16 | LUNCH BOX
Don't worry

Friday was the only good day to buy lunch in the cafeteria—they always served pizza on Fridays—so most of the time my friends and I brought our lunch from home. Some of them would bring their lunches to school in a brown lunch bag, but I had a metal lunch box with my favorite superhero on it—Spiderman. Spiderman was amazing.

Whether you bring your lunch in a paper bag, metal lunch box or buy lunch at school, eating is an important part of the day. Most people in America have very few days when they are forced to skip a meal. Most people you know have never gone hungry because there wasn't enough food. In fact, we have an excess of food in this country and throw away a lot of good food every day, because we're full or just don't happen to like it. Food is a necessary part of life, and eating lunch gives your body the necessary energy to make it through the rest of the day. When you miss a meal, you might feel as though you're about ready to starve to death or have less energy than normal.

As important as food is, you probably don't worry too much about where your next meal is coming from. You know that your mom will cook dinner, you'll grab something on your own or you'll go out to a restaurant to eat. But you might worry about other things. Like how you look. Or if your friends will accept you. Or if that special guy or girl really likes you. You might worry about your grades, getting zits or what to wear. You might worry about the future, the past, your next class or your next doctor's appointment. Do you ever worry about your mistakes, successes and your reputation? You could probably add to the list.

Whenever I reached into my locker and pulled out my Spiderman lunch box, I didn't have to worry about having enough to eat. I knew that my mom had prepared a lunch for me that would satisfy my hunger. God wants us to trust him like that in every aspect of our lives. He doesn't want us to worry at all. He promises that he'll take care of us. Try to give all your worries to him and just enjoy the life he's given you.

HITTING THE BOOK

Read Matthew 6:25-34. In verse 33 Jesus promises that his Father will take care of those who follow him. What are the top three things you worry about?

_____

_____

_____

_____

_____

_____

How will your worrying affect their outcome?

_____

_____

_____

_____

LESSONS LEARNED

What do you think God is trying to tell you today?

_____

_____

_____

_____

_____

_____

_____

_____

_____

TODAY'S ASSIGNMENT

How can you deal with your worries today?

_____

_____

_____

_____

_____

_____

_____

_____

_____

_____

TALKING TO GOD

Take some time to ask God to help you live this out. What do you need to say to him today?

_____

_____

_____

_____

_____

_____

_____

_____

_____

_____

OTHER THOUGHTS

_____

_____

_____

_____

_____

_____

_____

_____

_____

_____

DAY 17 | GYM CLOTHES
Get in shape spiritually

At the school I went to, we were required to take physical education every day. So every morning I'd put clean PE clothes in my backpack and head off to school. Each night when I got home, I'd drop those dirty, smelly, damp clothes down the laundry chute to get washed. I tried really hard to remember to take home my used PE clothes each day because when I didn't, my locker began to smell like something had died in it.

PE class gave me an opportunity to have fun, compete with others and release some of my pent-up energy. I loved to play all sports, especially basketball, football and soccer, and I was on the wrestling and soccer teams. I liked PE class when we were playing team sports, but I wasn't really into working out like some people at my school.

We had a weight-lifting area in the athletic building that we referred to as The Cage. In it was a series of free weights and benches surrounded by a chain-link fence to keep the stuff from getting stolen. There were some guys who really got into weight lifting. They lifted weights four or five days a week and bought special workout clothes and shoes. They took vitamins and protein drinks to improve their health—they were really into it. Every day before and after school, guys would gather at The Cage to work out. These were hard-core weight-lifting guys. They would be at school at six in the morning to lift and not leave until six in the evening, after lifting again.

Within this group of weight lifters, there was an inner group. These guys were members of the 1,000 Pound Club. To become a member, a student had to do three different types of lifts—bench press, squats and curls—and the total weight had to be at least 1,000 pounds. The prize for getting into the club was the applause of friends and a yellow T-shirt that said 1,000 Pound Club Member.

The guys who made it into the club were proud of their physical strength and for being part of an exclusive club.

Some people put a lot of time, effort and priority into how strong and in shape their bodies can become. But you don't have to live very long to realize that your body won't last forever. Bones break. Muscles ache. And eventually you'll lose your speed. There are things that last longer than your physical body. Those are the things you need to focus on.

HITTING THE BOOK

First Timothy 4:8 says, "Exercise daily in God—no spiritual flabbiness, please! Workouts in the gymnasium are useful, but a disciplined life in God is far more so, making you fit both today and forever" (*Message*).

The apostle Paul says that physical training is of some value. But what is more valuable? A disciplined life in God. The goal is to strive to be more like God every day. What does this mean to you?

_____

_____

_____

_____

_____

_____

_____

_____

_____

LESSONS LEARNED

Think and write about one area in which you need to be more like God.

_____

_____

_____

_____

_____

_____

_____

_____

_____

_____

_____

What are some ungodly areas you need to work on? How can you do this?

_____

_____

_____

_____

_____

_____

_____

_____

_____

_____

_____

What kinds of exercises for God have you been neglecting?

_____

_____

_____

_____

_____

_____

_____

_____

_____

Why is it important to stay in good shape spiritually?

_____

_____

_____

_____

_____

_____

_____

_____

_____

_____

_____

_____

TODAY'S ASSIGNMENT

How can you get in shape for God today?

_____

_____

_____

_____

_____

_____

_____

_____

_____

_____

List three spiritual exercises you can do this week.

_____

_____

_____

_____

_____

_____

_____

_____

_____

_____

TALKING TO GOD

Take a few minutes to pray and ask God to help you remember today's lesson and carry it with you throughout the day.

_____

_____

_____

_____

_____

_____

_____

_____

_____

OTHER THOUGHTS

_____

_____

_____

_____

_____

_____

_____

_____

_____

DAY 18 | HOOKS
Be kind to others

Even though no one has ever come by to check out the hooks in your locker, no locker is complete without a couple of hooks. Hooks are usually fairly inconspicuous—you might not really notice them until one breaks or falls out of your locker. Maybe that's because they're intended to be functional, not stylish—they're designed to hold things and that's about it. They silently do their job without drawing attention to themselves, but it sure is helpful to have them around.

Jessica was a girl in my school who was kind of like the hooks in a locker. She was kind and compassionate and never did anything to draw attention to herself. She always did good things for people and never desired any thanks or repayment—she loved it when she could do something nice for someone without them finding out that she was the one who had done it. She practiced "random acts of kindness" long before Oprah made them popular.

Jessica had a goal to do one kind act for someone each day. The cool thing about it was that Jessica didn't just do kind things for her friends and family—she did kind things for people who would probably never do anything kind for her in return. She did kind things for the elderly, for popular kids and even for kids whom everyone else made fun of.

We had a group of special education students in our high school who were physically or mentally disabled or both. They all rode to school on a special bus that was shorter than the other buses. As you can imagine, this group was made fun of and picked on a lot by the other students.

One of the special education students was a boy named Jared, who had cerebral palsy. Even though his mind was fully functioning, because of his disability he was part of this special group of students. He had a hard time getting around because of his disease—standing, walking and talking were difficult challenges at best.

One particular morning as I was waiting for a friend to get to school, the "short bus" pulled up, and the students slowly began to get off the bus. It was a long process—some of them were in wheelchairs and had to be helped by the bus driver. Jared struggled to get down the steps of the bus. As he got to the last step, he must have tripped or something, because he fell facedown onto the driveway. His books and papers went flying.

It was obvious that Jared was embarrassed—who wouldn't be? The worst part was that no one made a move to help him. We just stood around making snappy comments and snickering at his expense. As he hurried the best he could to collect his things before shuffling off to first hour, Jessica happened to walk by. It didn't take her long to figure out what had happened. When the bus pulled away, she noticed that Jared had missed a notebook that had fallen under the bus. Jessica picked up the notebook and wiped off the dirt as best she could. She hurried after Jared and slipped the crumpled notebook into his backpack.

Jared never did find out what Jessica had done for him. And Jessica probably never knew that she had at least doubled her random acts of kindness quota that day. When I saw her grab the notebook and return it to Jared—all without judging the rest of us—I realized that she was living like Jesus calls us to live. I finally recognized that even though I acted like a Christian on Sundays, I was spending most of my time trying to build myself up instead of others. I still struggle with that almost every day, but I'm slowly learning to be an encouragement to others. Thanks, Jessica!

HITTING THE BOOK

First Thessalonians 5:11 reminds us to "encourage one another and build each other up, just as in fact you are doing." Also read Matthew 6:1-4. Jesus says when we help others, we should do it without drawing attention to ourselves. What do these verses mean to you?

_____

_____

_____

_____

_____

_____

_____

LESSONS LEARNED

Has anyone ever done anything out of the ordinary or special for you without expecting anything in return?

_____

_____

_____

_____

_____

_____

_____

What was it?

_____

_____

_____

_____

_____

_____

_____

_____

_____

Have you ever done a random act of kindness for someone? How did
that feel? What happened?

_____

_____

_____

_____

_____

_____

_____

_____

_____

_____

_____

TODAY'S ASSIGNMENT

How can you do an unseen act of kindness for someone today?

TALKING TO GOD

Ask God to help you let his love shine through you today. What do you need to talk with him about?

OTHER THOUGHTS

DAY 19 | MAGNETS
God wants to hang out with you

My grandmother had a habit of collecting magnets. She put them on the door of her refrigerator. When the grandkids came over, we'd end up at the door of the fridge arranging and rearranging the magnets. We often made pretend roads for our Matchbox® cars to drive on. Sometimes we created pictures with the magnets. But we eventually grew out of our magnet phase.

However, there was a group of girls who shared a locker pretty close to mine in school who probably still haven't tired of playing with magnets. There must have been four or five girls who used the same locker. Like my Grandma, they collected magnets. At the beginning of the year they decided that they wanted to collect as many magnets as they could during the school year. They brought them to school and placed them inside their locker. Their goal was to cover the entire interior of their locker with little magnets.

So the girls set out in search of magnets. They bought some from stores, took others from their refrigerators at home and managed to find some free ones as well. Over the course of the year, they were able to completely cover the inside of their locker with the magnets. They covered the door, the walls, even the floor, shelf and ceiling! There must have been three or four hundred magnets inside. I have to admit that the locker looked pretty cool with all the different colors, shapes and sizes of magnets. Other students were always coming by to see the inside of their locker.

Magnets are great for more than just their aesthetic value though. They are a reminder of the principle that opposites attract. The positive and negative atoms line up and create a magnetic field. I don't fully understand all the specifics of a magnet, but I do know that they are fun to play with. I even created my own temporary magnet in science class.

The principle of opposites attracting is also true in the Christian life. God is perfect. He has never made a mistake. On the other hand, people make mistakes all the time. We sin every day. The great thing about God is that, although he is perfect and we are very imperfect, he wants to be with us. Opposites attract!

HITTING THE BOOK

In John 12:32 Jesus predicted, "But I, when I am lifted up from the earth, will draw all men to myself." Jesus knew that he was going to be crucified. He literally would be lifted up on the cross. But he was also speaking about how his crucifixion and resurrection would stand out in history as the most incredible God-event of all time by bringing people back into relationships with him.

Jesus wants opposites to attract. The perfect God wants to spend time with you. What is one way you can spend quality time with him today?

LESSONS LEARNED

What is God trying to tell you through his Word today?

_____

_____

_____

_____

_____

_____

_____

_____

_____

TODAY'S ASSIGNMENT

What are some practical ways in which you can draw closer to him today?

_____

_____

_____

_____

_____

_____

_____

_____

_____

TALKING TO GOD

Take some time to thank God for his desire to be close to you. Thank
him for what Jesus did to draw you to himself.

_____

_____

_____

_____

_____

_____

_____

_____

_____

OTHER THOUGHTS

_____

_____

_____

_____

_____

_____

_____

_____

_____

_____

DAY 20 | NOTEBOOKS
Live for God every day

Most students have a notebook for each class they're taking. You might have a notebook for math, another for science, still another for English or a foreign language and other subjects you're taking. When you go to class, you grab the appropriate notebook to take notes, keep track of assignments and keep yourself entertained. As the semester progresses, each notebook gets filled with information that is vital for passing the class.

Notebooks come in various sizes, styles, colors and formats, from the cheap wire-bound notebooks that come unraveled to the perfectly bound notebooks with perforated paper. There are even elaborate notebook systems that keep a set of notebooks together and provide the option of taking each notebook out individually to make it easier to keep track of an entire semester's coursework.

I didn't have one of those notebook systems, but I thought they were cool. Maybe that's why I finally realized that I had compartmentalized my life like a series of separate notebooks. When I was at school, I pulled out my school notebook and did whatever I wanted. But when I was at church, I pulled out my church notebook and lived according to that plan. At times it was hard to live both lives, but I figured that I could have the best of both worlds.

I vividly remember the day that my elaborate system came crashing down around me. My teacher somehow got onto the subject of religion and asked if anyone in the class considered himself a Christian. I raised my hand, to the surprise of several people in the class. You see, I was a master at playing the game. I was a leader in my church's youth group and a great student in front of my parents. But at school in front of my non-Christian friends, I was completely the opposite. I would do anything to fit in with my friends. If that meant cussing, I cussed. If that meant lying, I lied. Whatever it took to fit in, I did.

That day in social studies class, my two worlds collided, and I began to realize that I had a problem in my life. I was trying to live two lives. I was one person at home and at church. I was the opposite when I was with my friends. I knew from that moment on that I was going to have to live my life from one notebook or the other. Fortunately, I decided to live my life for God. It wasn't easy. I lost some of my friendships because of the choices I began to make. But in the long run, it was definitely worth it.

HITTING THE BOOK

Read Luke 9:23-27. Two phrases from Jesus' strong words in these verses really stand out: "take up [your] cross daily and follow me," and, "If anyone is ashamed of me and my words, the Son of Man will be ashamed of him when he comes in his glory."

Taking up your cross daily refers to the sacrifice Jesus made for you on the cross. Living for him requires some sacrifice on your part. If you are ashamed of Jesus here on earth, the gloomy promise in these words is that he will be ashamed of you on judgment day. What do these words mean to you?

LESSONS LEARNED

What have you sacrificed for God lately?

_____

_____

_____

_____

_____

_____

_____

_____

_____

_____

_____

Was it a willing sacrifice? Why or why not?

_____

_____

_____

_____

_____

_____

_____

_____

_____

_____

Have you been ashamed of your belief in Christ recently? Why?

_____

_____

_____

_____

_____

_____

_____

_____

Do you ever find yourself being two different people depending on who you are with? Describe your experience.

_____

_____

_____

_____

_____

_____

_____

_____

_____

_____

_____

TODAY'S ASSIGNMENT

How can you "take up your cross" for Christ today?

_____

_____

_____

_____

_____

_____

_____

_____

_____

_____

Name three areas of your life where you need to take a stronger stand for Christ.

_____

_____

_____

_____

_____

_____

_____

_____

_____

TALKING TO GOD

Ask God to help you deal with this profound truth today. What do you
need to talk with him about?

_____

_____

_____

_____

_____

_____

_____

_____

_____

OTHER THOUGHTS

_____

_____

_____

_____

_____

_____

_____

_____

DAY 21 | MAKEUP

Jesus improves your appearance

Because our school was growing, one summer a row of new lockers was added to a hallway. One of these lockers had an unusual feature. There was an electrical outlet on the wall, and whoever had installed the lockers made a cutout in the back of one of the lockers for it.

The first person to use that locker was a girl named Amy. She loved the fact that her locker had an outlet in the back wall, and she sure took advantage of it! Amy brought in her lighted makeup mirror and curling iron and set up a salon that she and her friends used each morning. Her locker contained hairbrushes, nail polish, lip gloss, hair spray, hand lotion, lipstick, makeup, barrettes, hair bows and headbands. It was really amazing to see how much stuff she could fit inside that locker.

When I arrived at school and walked the halls each morning, there was always a crowd of girls around Amy's locker. I saw them curling their hair, talking about girl stuff and sharing makeup tips with each other. (OK, I really don't know what they talked about, but that's what my friends and I thought they were doing.) They thought it was the best locker in the world, but I just thought that it was hilarious.

Seeing how excited Amy and her friends were about constantly modifying their appearances made me realize that there aren't too many girls who go with the "all natural" look. Most females use makeup every day to hide imperfections such as an untimely zit or tired eyes. It hides the bad stuff and makes girls look prettier on the outside. If a student is having a bad-hair day, hairspray, gel or mousse can make it look better. If she doesn't smell just right a little perfume can cover it up.

If you think about it, Jesus does the same thing for us on the inside. By ourselves, we are prone to make mistakes, leaving ourselves ugly with sin. But Jesus forgives our sin and wipes away the ugliness. He makes us look better than we do in our sins.

HITTING THE BOOK

Romans 5:8, 9 says, "But God showed his great love for us by sending Christ to die for us while we were still sinners. And since we have been made right in God's sight by the blood of Christ, he will certainly save us from God's judgment" (NLT). See also 2 Corinthians 5:21.

Jesus made you "right in God's sight" by his blood. His death has given you the opportunity to trade your sins for his goodness. What a deal! When you appear before God on judgment day, you stand guilty of your sins, but Jesus' blood wipes them all away. If you have accepted the free gift of salvation from him, you'll stand before God with a clean slate, because Jesus has forgiven you. What is one way God's forgiveness makes you appear better than you are?

_____

_____

_____

_____

_____

_____

_____

LESSONS LEARNED

What is God trying to tell you through his Word today?

_____

_____

_____

_____

_____

_____

_____

_____

_____

_____

TODAY'S ASSIGNMENT

What are some practical ways you can live like you've been forgiven?

_____

_____

_____

_____

_____

_____

_____

_____

_____

_____

_____

TALKING TO GOD

Take some time to thank God for Jesus' sacrifice that made forgiveness possible for you. What else do you need to talk with him about today?

_____

_____

_____

_____

_____

_____

_____

_____

_____

OTHER THOUGHTS

_____

_____

_____

_____

_____

_____

_____

_____

_____

DAY 22 | BIBLE
Don't be ashamed of God

One year my youth group went on a weekend retreat at our church camp. I was excited about the retreat because I always loved going to church camp, but I knew that this wasn't going to be like a regular week of camp. For one thing, I was used to being at the camp during the summer, but it was almost wintertime. We stayed inside most of the time because of the cold weather and didn't once venture out into the lake. Instead of being a weeklong camp, this was just a three-day weekend retreat. There weren't any new people from different churches to meet because our youth group was the only one there.

In spite of all the differences, I was ready for a great retreat. Our youth minister brought in a special speaker. I don't know exactly why, but I really related to this guy. It seemed to me that when he spoke, he was speaking right to me. For once in my life, I didn't get bored with the talk, and I actually took notes on some of the stuff he was saying.

I remember him speaking on Sunday morning just before we all headed back home. He said that when he was in junior high and senior high, he was a Christian—but he was a "closet Christian." He said that almost none of his friends knew that he was a Christian or even that he went to church! He then talked about Jesus' sacrificial death on the cross. In vivid detail he described exactly what happened during Jesus' crucifixion. Even though it was kind of gross, the depiction made me think about all that Jesus had gone through for me.

Then the speaker challenged us to live for Jesus. He said that after all Christ had endured and done for us so that we could live with him forever in Heaven, it was the least that we could do. That day I decided to start carrying my Bible to school every day—a huge step for me at the time.

So the next day I headed off to school with my Bible in my backpack. On my way to school, I started to get nervous and scared. *What would my friends think and say?* I wondered. My fear increased exponentially as I got closer to school. When I arrived at my locker, I decided that I had done a lot just by bringing my Bible to school—even though no one had seen it in my backpack—so I slipped it quietly into my locker and escaped to my first class.

I thought that I had shelved the whole Bible issue, but I was completely miserable during that class. I felt guilty about all that Jesus had done for me, and how I was too embarrassed to carry a Bible at school. So I gathered my courage, pulled my Bible out of my locker and took it to second period. I did get some funny looks from my friends, but nothing really terrible happened. I even had a couple people tell me that they thought it was great that I had my Bible with me. And I felt as though I was taking a stand, in a small way, for God.

HITTING THE BOOK

In Romans 1:16 the apostle Paul declared, "I am not ashamed of the gospel, because it is the power of God for the salvation of everyone who believes: first for the Jew, then for the Gentile."

Do you agree with Paul's words?

_____

_____

_____

_____

_____

LESSONS LEARNED

Some students demonstrate that they are ashamed of God by their actions. They might be afraid to wear Christian T-shirts, listen to Christian music, talk about Jesus or invite their friends to church or youth group. How do you feel about this?

_____

_____

_____

_____

_____

_____

_____

_____

_____

_____

Was there ever a time when you were nervous to reveal that you are a Christian? When?

_____

_____

_____

_____

_____

_____

_____

_____

_____

_____

_____

Why were you nervous?

What helps you to not be ashamed of the gospel?

TODAY'S ASSIGNMENT

How can you live Paul's words out at school today?

_____

_____

_____

_____

_____

_____

_____

_____

_____

_____

Write down two challenges for yourself—ways you can tell or show others what you believe.

_____

_____

_____

_____

_____

_____

_____

_____

_____

_____

_____

_____

TALKING TO GOD

Pray for an opportunity to stand up for God today. Get ready—God *will* answer your prayer!

_____

_____

_____

_____

_____

_____

_____

_____

_____

_____

OTHER THOUGHTS

_____

_____

_____

_____

_____

_____

_____

_____

DAY 23 | CELL PHONE
God is always with you

A girl in our youth group named Lauren came to me one day showing off her Christmas present—a brand new cell phone. She had wanted one for months and had begged her parents to get it for her for Christmas. All of her friends had had cell phones since the beginning of the school year, and she had been feeling like she was on the outside. She was excited about always having a phone with her and being able to talk to her friends whenever she wanted.

When I asked her about what she could do with her phone, she began to rattle off a list of uses: calling friends between classes, ordering pizza in for lunch, calling her mom about last-minute after school plans, being able to call her boyfriend whenever she wanted, and being able to snap photos and send text messages. Lauren was elated that no matter where she was, she could call almost anyone at any time. She loved the feeling of being connected.

The next week when I saw Lauren, I asked her how life with her phone was going. She wasn't nearly as excited as she had been the week before. Evidently there was a new rule at her school that no one was allowed to use a cell phone during school hours, unless it was an emergency. Students weren't even allowed to carry them to class. Lauren had to leave her phone turned off and in her locker all day. Now she couldn't call her friends, order a pizza or do any of the other things she had been so excited about doing. She wasn't too happy about the situation.

Lauren didn't know what she was going to do, because she was upset that she felt cut off from her friends. Sometimes you may feel that way about God. You know he exists. You know he's every-where. You just wish that you could touch, see or hear from him once in a while. But God's promises are true. He promised 3,500 years ago in the book of Deuteronomy that he'd never leave you. That promise still stands true today.

HITTING THE BOOK

As Moses was passing the mantle of leadership to Joshua, he spoke these awesome words to the children of Israel: "The Lord will deliver them to you, and you must do to them all that I have commanded you. Be strong and courageous. Do not be afraid or terrified because of them, for the Lord your God goes with you; he will never leave you nor forsake you" (Deuteronomy 31:5, 6). How does it make you feel to know that God will never leave you?

_____

_____

_____

_____

_____

Has knowing God is with you ever helped you to be strong? How?

_____

_____

_____

_____

_____

_____

LESSONS LEARNED

What things are you doing to stay connected to God? Are they working?

_____

_____

_____

_____

_____

_____

_____

_____

_____

_____

TODAY'S ASSIGNMENT

What is one way you can "reach out and touch" him today?

_____

_____

_____

_____

_____

_____

_____

_____

_____

TALKING TO GOD

Jeremiah 33:3 says that God is always willing for you to call him up and talk. What do you need to say to him today?

_____

_____

_____

_____

_____

_____

_____

_____

_____

_____

OTHER THOUGHTS

_____

_____

_____

_____

_____

_____

_____

_____

_____

DAY 24 | PROJECTS
Be prepared to answer

Whenever a teacher assigned a major project at the beginning of the semester, I always got a little nervous. I knew that it would require a lot of work, and I also knew that it would be worth a large part of our final grade. But the thing that scared me the most was presenting the project to the class when all of the work was finally done. The thought of standing up and talking in front of my peers scared me to death!

So you can imagine how I felt when my science teacher informed our class that we would be working with a partner to illustrate a scientific law and then present the project to the class. My friend Steve and I got to be partners. He wasn't any more excited about the presentation than I was, but we were both excited about the project itself. Steve and I decided that we would prove the validity of the second law of thermodynamics. The second law of thermodynamics states, "In a closed system, things left to themselves will increase in entropy." To increase in entropy means to become less organized or to decay.

Steve and I decided to show how when a part of a living plant is cut off, it will decay over time. We cut a small fruit-bearing branch from an apple tree, placed the limb inside a plastic garbage can, and sealed it tightly. We set the can outside my garage and checked it every other day to record what had happened. Over the course of a few weeks, the branch and fruit turned brown and began to rot and smell. By the end of the two months, we could hardly stand to open the can because of the smell. At the end of the experiment, the leaves resembled dirt, having almost completely decomposed. But our project did prove that when something is left to itself, it gets worse, not better.

After we collected the data, we had to decide how we would present it to the class. We decided to mount samples of a branch that had been cut at staggered times—one day, one week, four weeks, eight weeks and twelve weeks. On the day of our presentation, we stood before the class and illustrated the second law of thermodynamics. After our presentation, students asked us questions, and we answered them with relative ease.

We got an A on the project, so it was worth all of the effort. The hardest part had actually been getting the project to school without ruining it! Standing before our class, giving our presentation and answering questions about our research was only possible because of one thing—Steve and I had studied and worked hard to be ready for our presentation. In a similar way, God wants you to be prepared to talk about your belief in him.

HITTING THE BOOK

If someone asks you why you believe and follow Jesus, do you have a better response than "My youth pastor, leader or parent told me to"? God wants you to be ready to present his case before anyone who asks you. First Peter 3:15 says "Through thick and thin, keep your hearts at attention, in adoration before Christ, your Master. Be ready to speak up and tell anyone who asks why you're living the way you are, and always with the utmost courtesy" (*Message*).

In what area of your Christian life do you need to prepare to answer some tough questions?

_____

_____

_____

_____

LESSONS LEARNED

What is God speaking to you today?

_____

_____

_____

_____

_____

_____

_____

_____

_____

_____

TODAY'S ASSIGNMENT

Look for an opportunity to answer for your faith in Christ today. Are there a few friends, family members or co-workers he wants you to talk with about him?

_____

_____

_____

_____

_____

_____

_____

_____

TALKING TO GOD

Ask God to open doors of opportunity today—then be ready when he answers. What do you need to tell him today?

_____

_____

_____

_____

_____

_____

_____

_____

_____

_____

OTHER THOUGHTS

_____

_____

_____

_____

_____

_____

_____

_____

DAY 25 | KEYS
Seek first God's kingdom

The keys someone carries say a lot about a person. Things that are the most important to someone are usually locked and require a key to get to. You might carry a key to your house, another key for a bike lock, a key for a diary or for your locker. People want to protect the things they care about. They usually do that by locking them up. The keys people carry are usually a pretty good representation of their priorities.

If you don't have to carry keys yet, think about your mom's or dad's key chain. They probably have keys to the house, the cars, their workplace and possibly a shed or storage facility. The things that are important to them are locked up and they carry keys to those items with them all the time.

Sometimes we get our priorities out of order. We get all upset if something happens to our house, bike, diary or locker. Sometimes we pay more attention to these things than we do to other people. We get so consumed with our stuff that we forget about the people who matter most to us.

I remember one time when my brother took my bike without asking me. Of course he got caught when he wrecked it on the street and skinned up his knee and elbow pretty badly. The concrete also made a little tear in the seat of my bike. I was so mad at him for taking my bike without asking and for tearing the seat that I didn't care that he was in pain and bleeding.

What was going on? Where were my priorities? It took me a while to realize that my priorities were out of whack. I had placed the value of my bike over the health of my brother. Somewhere along the way I had stopped trusting God to provide for me what I really need, and I was getting uptight about circumstances I couldn't control.

HITTING THE BOOK

In Matthew 6:32, 33, Jesus says to you, "Why be like the pagans who are so deeply concerned about these things? Your heavenly Father already knows all your needs, and he will give you all you need from day to day if you live for him and make the Kingdom of God your primary concern" (*NLT*).

God challenges you to seek his kingdom first, and he'll take care of the rest. What are some things that you care about more than other people?

_____

_____

_____

_____

_____

_____

_____

Why do you think that you care so much about those things?

_____

_____

_____

_____

_____

_____

_____

LESSONS LEARNED

What is God saying to you today?

_____

_____

_____

_____

_____

_____

_____

_____

_____

_____

TODAY'S ASSIGNMENT

What are some practical ways in which you can seek his purposes first today?

_____

_____

_____

_____

_____

_____

_____

_____

_____

_____

TALKING TO GOD

Take a few minutes to pray and ask God to help you remember today's lesson and carry it with you throughout the day.

_____

_____

_____

_____

_____

_____

_____

_____

_____

_____

_____

OTHER THOUGHTS

_____

_____

_____

_____

_____

_____

_____

_____

DAY 26 | PEN AND PENCIL
Be thankful

Jake was a student at my school who was known for collecting pencils. It might seem like an odd hobby, but he was always ordering new pencils and showing off his newest set. His favorite was an NFL set; it contained a pencil with the logo of every professional football team in the NFL. People probably thought that Jake was a little weird because he was so into pencils, but they were always glad when he was around if they needed a pencil in a hurry.

Though you probably don't get as excited about pencils as Jake did, no doubt you have a variety of pens and pencils in your locker that you use every day to write all kinds of things. Think about all the different things you write in the course of a day. You write assignments, notes to your friends, to-do lists, class notes and many other things.

Without a pen or pencil, it would be difficult to do any of that, but you probably don't worry too much about having a pen or pencil. If you don't have one with you, you can usually find one or borrow one from a friend or someone who sits next to you in class. Pens and pencils are cheap and easy to find—companies even hand out free pens to advertise new products.

The actual pen or pencil usually doesn't hold much value. The real value in a pen or pencil is in how it is used—the words that you write with your pen or pencil are the important thing. You can write words that are good and you can write words that are destructive. You can write things that make people feel better about themselves and things that make them feel bad.

When I was growing up, my mom always made me write thank-you notes to everyone who gave me a gift. I was not allowed to spend any money or use my gift until I had written a note to the giver.

I used to hate writing the notes, but now I don't mind it as much because I love it when someone sends me a note.

Why not use your pen or pencil today to thank or encourage someone you appreciate or someone who has recently done something for you? You won't believe the difference it will make in his or her life!

HITTING THE BOOK

The apostle Paul advises in 1 Timothy 4:4: "Everything God created is good, and to be received with thanks. Nothing is to be sneered at and thrown out" (*Message*).

You really are fortunate. I don't mean that you don't have any problems; I mean that God has given you a lot to be thankful for. You have a place to live, clothes to wear and food to eat. You are better off than 50 percent of the world. Everything and everyone that God has created is good. What things are you thankful for?

_____

_____

_____

_____

_____

_____

_____

_____

_____

Who is someone that you are thankful for?

_____

_____

_____

_____

_____

_____

_____

_____

_____

LESSONS LEARNED

Thanksgiving is much more than just a holiday. What is God saying
about giving thanks?

_____

_____

_____

_____

_____

_____

_____

_____

_____

What things do you forget to be thankful for?

_____

_____

_____

_____

_____

_____

_____

_____

_____

Have you ever "thrown out" something that was good?

_____

_____

_____

_____

_____

_____

_____

_____

_____

_____

_____

TODAY'S ASSIGNMENT

In what practical ways can you apply today's lesson to your life?

_____

_____

_____

_____

_____

_____

_____

_____

_____

Can you get specific and name at least five things and five people you thank God for?

_____

_____

_____

_____

_____

_____

_____

_____

_____

_____

TALKING TO GOD

Spend some time today thanking God for who he is and for what his
Son has done for you. Ask him to make you a more grateful person.

_____

_____

_____

_____

_____

_____

_____

_____

_____

_____

OTHER THOUGHTS

_____

_____

_____

_____

_____

_____

_____

_____

_____

DAY 27 | MONEY
Love people, not stuff

Whether we like it or not, money plays a big role in our lives. We spend money on clothes, eating, drinking, getting to school and all kinds of entertainment and leisure activities. There's a constant danger of money becoming a bit too important to us. There are some people who never seem to have enough.

You probably know someone at school who is always asking people for money. At my school that was Jamie. Jamie knew that I kept some change in my locker in case I needed to make a phone call—I wasn't cool enough to have my own cell phone—and every day he asked if he could use that money to buy a drink. I rarely gave him any money, but he kept asking. Jamie had no qualms about asking someone to share lunch money or even earnings from a fund-raiser when there was something he wanted to buy.

One day a group of my friends and I decided to find out what Jamie was willing to do to get a few dollars so we devised a plan. We mixed up a nasty stew of cafeteria leftovers—bread crusts, red Kool Aid®, green beans, milk, hot sauce, chocolate chip cookies and anything else we could find—and told Jamie that we'd give him twelve dollars if he ate it.

Of course Jamie accepted the challenge. So we placed the money on the table and handed him a large spoon. He looked at the money, then at the mixture and then back at the money. He picked up the spoon and took his first bite. His eyes got really big as he swallowed, but he kept the concoction down. He crammed down the nasty leftovers, grabbed the money and ran to the bathroom. He had done it.

Everyone gathered at the table had a good laugh at Jamie. We were amazed by what he was willing to do for a few dollars. We realized that he would stoop to do almost anything for cash because he loved money. He always wanted more.

HITTING THE BOOK

If you struggle with loving money read Luke 16:13. Take a look at 1 Timothy 6:10 too: "For the love of money is at the root of all kinds of evil. And some people, craving money, have wandered from the faith and pierced themselves with many sorrows" (NLT).

If money becomes a big part of your life, be aware that you can do some pretty dumb things because of it. There is a lot more to life than just money; happiness and contentment mean more over the long haul.

What are these verses saying to you?

_____

_____

_____

_____

_____

_____

_____

_____

_____

_____

_____

_____

LESSONS LEARNED

How important is money to you? Why?

_____

_____

_____

_____

_____

_____

_____

_____

_____

How important is having the newest, latest thing to you?

_____

_____

_____

_____

_____

_____

_____

_____

_____

_____

_____

_____

How low would you stoop for money?

_____

_____

_____

_____

_____

_____

_____

_____

_____

_____

Has the love of money or things ever caused you to wander from your faith? What happened?

_____

_____

_____

_____

_____

_____

_____

_____

_____

_____

_____

TODAY'S ASSIGNMENT

How can you turn over your attitude about things and money to God today?

_____

_____

_____

_____

_____

_____

_____

_____

Think of something you regularly spend money on. What is it? Write down three ways you could use this money for God instead.

_____

_____

_____

_____

_____

_____

_____

_____

_____

_____

TALKING TO GOD

Take some time to ask God to help you deal with money issues.

_____

_____

_____

_____

_____

_____

_____

_____

_____

_____

OTHER THOUGHTS

_____

_____

_____

_____

_____

_____

_____

_____

_____

_____

DAY 28 | HIDDEN STASH
Secret sins

One day a group of guys who didn't exactly have the best reputation around school were walking down the hall past my locker. They were laughing about something, and by the way they were acting I knew that they were up to no good. As it happened, they stopped at my locker and turned and looked at me. Mike, the leader of the group, stepped forward and asked if I'd like a drink of hot chocolate from his thermos.

Now I might not have been the smartest guy in school, but I knew a setup when I saw one, so I politely refused. They continued to press me to take a drink, and I kept refusing. Another student wandered by at that moment and the group of guys turned their attention to him. I got out of there as fast as I could.

I wondered about that situation all day. Then, during the last hour, one of my friends told me that he had heard that Mike had been suspended from school. He said that the principal had found alcohol in his locker—Mike had been hiding it in a thermos of hot chocolate. Boy, was I glad that I didn't take Mike up on his offer for a drink!

Mike made the mistake of bringing alcohol to school. It was against the rules. But how many times have students kept things in their lockers that were against school rules? Students have gotten caught with alcohol, cigarettes, a dirty magazine or video, drugs and even weapons in their lockers at school. Maybe you don't have anything bad in your locker, but what have you got stashed in your closet, in a box hidden under your bed, on your hard drive or in some secret hiding place?

At one time or another many of us keep something hidden that we know we shouldn't have, but for some reason we keep it. If our parents found it, they would be angry and disappointed. We might get in trouble and be grounded for a long time.

As you get older it is easy to carry on the bad practice of hiding bad things. It might not be contraband, but it could be a secret sin or harmful habit. It might not be alcohol or drugs, but it could be pornography on the Internet or some other kind of addiction.

No one plans to get caught up in something bad. It usually starts out small and then turns into a bad habit that can become controlling. The key to avoiding that road is to be honest with yourself from the beginning. Admit that what you're hiding is wrong. Then be honest with God. Confess to him your weakness and ask for his forgiveness and strength to overcome it in the power of his Spirit.

HITTING THE BOOK

Read 1 John 1:9 again. You read it earlier in this book, but it's a powerful verse. In Jeremiah 31:34 God promises, "I will forgive their wickedness and will remember their sins no more." Wow! Those are powerful promises. If we confess our sins, God is faithful and just, and he will forgive us from them. The only condition is that we confess. If we do that, he promises to forgive our sins. And when God forgives, he forgets.

What sin would you like God to forget about?

_____

_____

_____

_____

LESSONS LEARNED

How does it make you feel when you try to hide something bad you are doing?

_____

_____

_____

_____

_____

_____

_____

_____

_____

_____

Have you ever confessed a secret sin to God or to someone else. How did that feel?

_____

_____

_____

_____

_____

_____

_____

_____

Maybe you think you have nothing to hide. Look closer—are you sure? What do you think God is trying to tell you?

_____

_____

_____

_____

_____

_____

_____

_____

_____

_____

Is there anything that keeps you from confessing? If so, what is it?

_____

_____

_____

_____

_____

_____

_____

_____

_____

_____

TODAY'S ASSIGNMENT

What are some practical ways in which you need to deal with this truth from God's Word today?

_____

_____

_____

_____

_____

_____

_____

_____

_____

If you confess something to God today, write here how you feel about that.

_____

_____

_____

_____

_____

_____

_____

_____

_____

_____

Do you need to share a secret sin with a trusted adult in order to get some help? That person might be a parent, a teacher, a counselor, a youth leader or a pastor. Think of some people who could help you.

_____

_____

_____

_____

_____

TALKING TO GOD

Take some time to say to God what you need to. He is there and he is listening!

_____

_____

_____

_____

OTHER THOUGHTS

_____

_____

_____

DAY 29 | CDS
You are special to God

O ur school didn't allow us to use portable CD players during school hours, but we were allowed to listen to them before and after school and on the bus. We just had to keep them stored in our locker when school was in session.

Whenever one of my friends bought a new CD, he'd carry it with him throughout the day. When there was a break at the end of a class, he'd get out the CD and look at it, talk about the band or read the liner notes.

The great thing about a CD is that it contains a group's best work. They labor for months, writing and recording the album. The record company promotes it and makes videos of the best songs. Radio stations play their music and hopefully lots of people buy the CD.

When you buy a CD you are making an investment. You only want to buy the CDs that you like. Some people like classic rock. Others prefer top 40, grunge, ska, heavy metal or new-age music. There are even a few who like country music, but they aren't my close friends! When you bring your CDs to school and show them to your friends, you hope that they like the same music that you do. You probably keep your favorite CDs with you so that you can listen to them anytime you choose.

I still have the first CD that I ever bought. I keep it on a shelf at home. It brings back memories of listening to it in my room on my new stereo. No matter how many new CDs I get, I'll never get rid of the first one that I bought.

You may have never thought of this before, but you are like God's favorite CD, his prized possession. He loves you with all his heart. If God went to school, he'd carry a picture of you in his wallet to show his friends. If God had a refrigerator, your picture would be on it. God's love for you is described in many ways in the Bible. But know this, God loves you with everything that he has. He even sent his Son Jesus to live a perfect life and die a sacrificial death so that you would have the opportunity to spend eternity in Heaven with him.

HITTING THE BOOK

In the second to last book in the Old Testament, you'll find these words in Zechariah 2:8: "Whoever touches you touches the apple of his eye."

The prophet Zechariah, who was speaking to encourage the people who were rebuilding the temple, wrote this verse in about 500 B.C. It makes the statement that anyone who belongs to God is the apple of his eye. That's a phrase that parents use for a son or daughter they really love. In other words God really loves you like a son or daughter—you are very special to him. How does it feel to be special to God?

LESSONS LEARNED

What do you need to hear God say to you today?

TODAY'S ASSIGNMENT

How can you live today like you are the son or daughter of the king of the universe?

TALKING TO GOD

Take a few minutes to express your appreciation to God for the way he makes you feel special. Talk to him as a loving father.

_____

_____

_____

_____

_____

_____

_____

_____

_____

OTHER THOUGHTS

_____

_____

_____

_____

_____

_____

_____

DAY 30 | LETTER JACKET
You are God's ambassador

When an athlete letters in a sport, he or she usually buys a letter jacket and has the school's letter attached to it. Athletes are generally pretty proud of their school jackets, but there's also some responsibility that comes with wearing one. Being a team member involves representing the team in whatever the athlete does—being an ambassador for the school and the sport.

An article in our local newspaper told the story of how one student athlete represented his school. The headline read, "Unidentified Student Hero Saves Family of Five!" The story went on to tell about a family that was traveling home for Thanksgiving, when they were caught in a terrible snowstorm. Their minivan slid off the highway, down the embankment and turned over. An anonymous student, who was identified only as wearing a football jacket from a neighboring school, happened to be driving behind them and witnessed the whole incident. Apparently the boy stopped his car and ran down the bank to the van. When he arrived he found that no one was seriously hurt, but the daughter had hurt her arm and face.

The boy helped the family out of the van and called 911 on his cell phone. The family made its way up the slippery embankment and, within a couple of minutes, an ambulance had arrived. When he saw that the family was being taken care of, the student left so that he could get home to his own family. As the paramedics tended to the family, a policeman asked for details of the accident. They told him everything, including how a boy had helped them and called for emergency assistance.

The policeman wanted to talk to the boy, and the family wanted to thank him, but he had gone too quickly. The family didn't even know his name. They only remembered that he was wearing a football letter jacket from a local school. The family contacted the school to see if they could find out who the unknown hero was, but they never did.

We'll never know if that unidentified hero was a Christian or not. At the very least he was a good Samaritan. At most, he was an ambassador for Christ.

HITTING THE BOOK

In 2 Corinthians 5:20, the apostle Paul says, "We are Christ's ambassadors, and God is using us to speak to you. We urge you, as though Christ himself were here pleading with you, 'Be reconciled to God!'" (*NLT*).

As a Christian, you represent Jesus in all that you do. While you may not have many opportunities to save a life, you do have many smaller opportunities to show God's love to others. When people see your actions and attitudes, they should see Christ's attitudes reflected in you.

What kind of ambassador are you for God?

_____

_____

_____

_____

_____

_____

_____

What have you done recently to be a good ambassador for him?

LESSONS LEARNED
What is God saying to you today?

TODAY'S ASSIGNMENT

How can you apply this lesson today?

_____

_____

_____

_____

_____

_____

TALKING TO GOD

Ask God to help you live this out through the day. What do you need to say to him today?

_____

_____

_____

_____

_____

_____

OTHER THOUGHTS

_____

_____

_____

SCRIPTURE REFERENCES | IN BIBLICAL ORDER